30TH ANNIVERSARY

NOISES
from
Under the Rug

THE BARRY LOUIS POLISAR SONGBOOK

ILLUSTRATED BY MICHAEL G. STEWART

He Eats Asparagus,
Why Can't You Be That Way?

When - ev - er I am naugh - ty, when - ev - er I am bad, When-

ev - er I do some - thing to make my par - ents mad, Like the

time I bit the mail - man or left stuff on the floor, Mom - my

says, "Why can't you be just like the boy who lives next door?" _

chorus

He al - ways makes his bed and he al - ways eats his food, He likes his

it - ty, bit - ty sis - ter and he's nev - er ev - er rude, And when

I don't eat what's on my plate, my par - ents will say,

"He eats as - par - a - gus, why can't you be that way?"

words and music
© by Barry Louis Polisar

He's never dirty, he always takes a bath,
He loves to do his homework too, especially math.
At school he is an angel, he always sits up straight,
He's always very helpful and never comes in late.

chorus

He always says, "I'm sorry," "Excuse me," "Thank you," "Please,"
He always dresses nicely, not like me.
He's never spilt his milk, lost a glove or slammed a door,
Stuck out his tongue, giggled in school or left things on the floor.

chorus

He goes to bed at nine each night and brushes all his teeth,
And Mommy wishes I was him and that he was me.
I've never even seen him burp, he does what he is told,
But the boy next door is thirty-four years old.

chorus

I'm a 3-Toed, Triple-Eyed, Double-Jointed Dinosaur

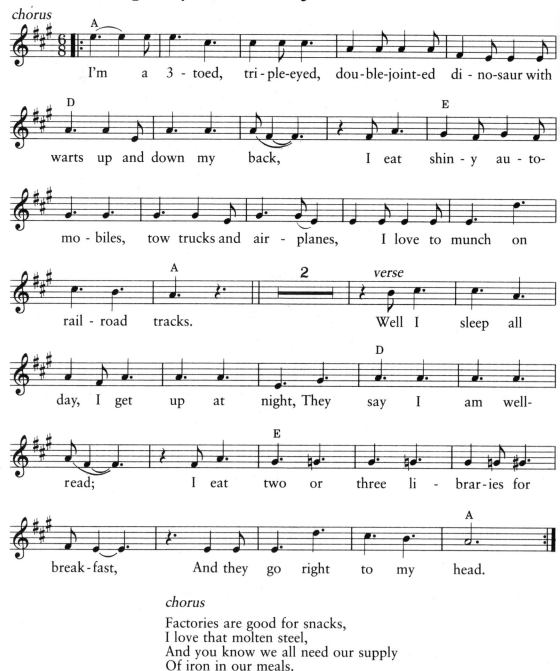

chorus

I'm a 3-toed, triple-eyed, double-jointed dinosaur with warts up and down my back, I eat shiny automobiles, tow trucks and airplanes, I love to munch on railroad tracks.

verse

Well I sleep all day, I get up at night, They say I am well-read; I eat two or three libraries for breakfast, And they go right to my head.

chorus

Factories are good for snacks,
I love that molten steel,
And you know we all need our supply
Of iron in our meals.

chorus

words and music
© by Barry Louis Polisar

I love to loaf, I love burnt toast,
Buttered asparagus too,
But the thing that I like most to eat
Is little kids just like you.

chorus

I've Got a Teacher, She's So Mean

I've got a teach - er, she's so mean, She nev - er laughs, she al - ways screams. She says, "Pay at - ten - tion" and, "Do what I said," But if you ask me, she's cra - zy in the head. Oh, she makes me ner - vous, she makes me squirm. She says, "All teach - ers must be firm."

chorus

And she al - ways calls on me when I don't raise my hand, So I an - swer her in ways that she can't un - der - stand. She says, "What is the an - swer to num - ber two?" I say, "Ak nak did - dy wop dick - ie pick - ie pooh." She says, "Don't be fun - ny, you'd bet - ter get it right." I say,

words and music
© by Barry Louis Polisar

"Shim-mie gim-mie gal-la gil-lie tack-ie tick-ie tie." She

She never lets us laugh, she never lets us smile,
"Wipe that grin off your face;" you're acting like a child."
It's "Work-work-work; no late papers today."
She's tired of excuses and yells at us all day.
She doesn't like children, she doesn't like kids,
Likes only regulations, and you know I never did.

chorus

I never see her laughing, she's so strict;
She never believes me me when I'm feeling sick.
She doesn't think it's funny when I fall off my chair.
And everybody knows that she's really unfair.
She can't understand me and I've got it made,
But I know she really loves me, 'cause I'm still in first grade.

chorus

When the House Is Dark and Quiet

Late at night when Mom - my and Dad - dy have gone out,

Me and my broth - er get to scream and jump and shout, 'Cause the

house is dark and qui - et and we're left all a - lone, With an -

oth - er teen - age ba - by - sit - ter talk - ing on the phone.

We tip - toe on our tip - toes and we

lis - ten to her laugh, While the wa - ter is run - ning so she

thinks we're in the bath. She tells her friend she's hun - gry so we

know just how to tease her; We go and get the

kit - ty - cat and hide it in the freez - er.

words and music
© by Barry Louis Polisar

Cindy opens up the door, you should have seen her leap,
Then we tell her, "That's the place where the kitty always sleeps."
She starts yelling then she sends us both to bed,
But Tim and me don't understand a single thing she says.
Assured that Tim and I are finally lying sound asleep,
She settles on the sofa and turns on the TV,
So Tim sneaks to the basement to disconnect the fuse,
While I am in the attic thumping in my father's shoes.
Cindy checks the TV set, examining the plug,
While I crawl across the living room underneath the rug.
We go and put the goldfish in the toilet bowl,
And spread strawberry jelly on on the toilet paper roll,
Standing on the sofa with carrots up our noses,
Pretending we are monsters, not wearing any clothes-es.
Cindy says she won't come back, just like Mike and Sue,
Melody and Barbara, John and Linda, too.
Mom and Dad can't leave us now, though we know that they must,
But we can't understand why no one wants to stay with us.

Our Dog Bernard

Our dog Bernard lived in the back-yard— Un-til one warm Ju-ly day, When our dog Ber-nard, who lived in the back-yard, De-cid-ed to run a-way.

He left a note taped to the front door: "I'm tired of this life," he said. "I'm tired of eat-ing dog-food (blech!) and get-ting chased off of the bed." Our

chorus

He ran off with the mailman
And is living with him now I hear,
Eating peanuts, pretzels and junk food,
Watching TV and drinking beer.

chorus

Oh Bernard, Bernard, please come back
Bernard you know that I love you.
I'll let you ride in the Cadillac,
I'll make it all up to you.

chorus

words and music
© by Barry Louis Polisar

Tomorrow

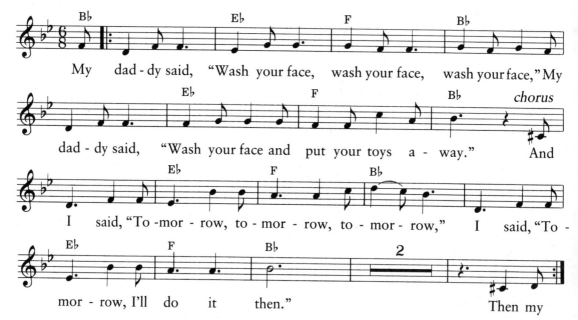

My dad-dy said, "Wash your face, wash your face, wash your face," My dad-dy said, "Wash your face and put your toys a - way." And I said, "To -mor - row, to - mor - row, to - mor - row," I said, "To - mor - row, I'll do it then." Then my

Then my mommy said, "Clean your room,"
"Clean your room," "Clean your room,"
My mommy said, "Clean your room,
And make your bed."

chorus

Then my uncle said, "Eat your food,
Eat your food, eat your food."
My uncle said, "Eat your food
And brush your teeth."

chorus

Then my grandpa said, "Take a bath,
Take a bath, take a bath."
My grandpa said, "Take a bath
And change your socks."

chorus

Then my grandma said, "Chocolate cake,
Chocolate cake, chocolate cake."
My grandma said, "Chocolate cake
And ice cream too."

chorus

And they all said, "Tomorrow, tomorrow, tomorrow."
They all said, "Tomorrow, you'll get it then."
Then I said, "Tomorrow, tomorrow, tomorrow,"
I said, "Tomorrow, I'll get it then."

words and music
© by Barry Louis Polisar

I Need You Like
a Donut Needs a Hole

chorus

I need you like a do-nut needs a hole, Like pi-an-os need fin-gers, heart and soul. We go to-geth-er like pea-nuts in a shell, I'm gon-na hold you in my arms like wa-ter in a well. And

And I love you like flowers love the sun,
Like birds love to fly and kids like to run,
Like trees love leaves and leaves turn brown,
Like rabbits in a meadow like to hop around.

chorus

When we are together, side by side,
It's like a roller coaster or a carousel ride.
The clouds all lift and sing with the trees,
The oak leaves dance along with the breeze.

chorus

words and music
© by Barry Louis Polisar

My Brother Threw Up
On My Stuffed Toy Bunny

My dad tried to help when I started to scream;
He threw my bunny in the washing machine,
But my bunny, Bill, still smelled so bad,
And I lost the best friend that I ever had.

chorus

words and music
© by Barry Louis Polisar

So bunny now sits on my shelf at home,
Next to the smelly toy telephone
And the dirty old bear with the stains and the spots,
'Cause my little brother throws up a lot.

chorus

Don't Put Your Finger
Up Your Nose

chorus

Don't put your fin - ger up your nose, 'Cause your

nose knows that's not the place it goes. You can

snif - fle, you can sneeze, But I'm ask - ing you, please,

Don't put your fin - ger up your nose.

Fine

verse

Don't stick your fin - ger in your ear, 'Cause

then your ear will find it hard to hear. You can

thump and you can tug it, But please, don't plug it,

1.,2.,3.

Don't stick your fin - ger in your ear.

D.C. al Fine

words and music
© by Barry Louis Polisar

chorus

Don't put your finger in your eye,
That's not a thing I think you oughta try.
You can blink it, you can wink it,
But I don't think it
Would be good to put your finger in your eye.

chorus

Don't stick your finger down your throat,
'Cause that will just make you start to choke.
Then up will come your dinner,
And you'll start to look much thinner,
Don't stick your finger down your throat.

chorus

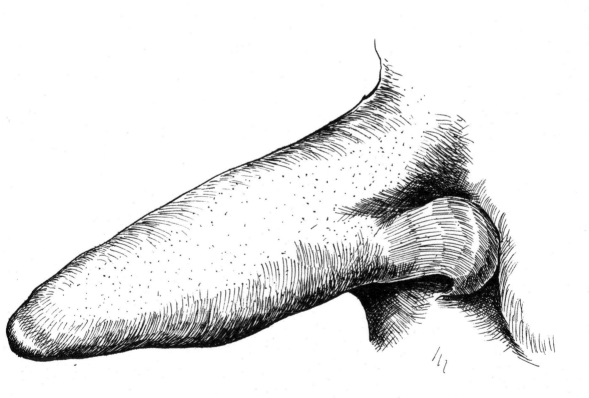

It's My Mother and My Father and My Sister and the Dog and My Two Little Brothers and Me

Oh, it's my moth-er and my fa-ther and my sis-ter and the dog and my two lit-tle broth-ers and me. We're go-ing on a trip and we're rid-ing in the car, we've been driv-ing all day it seems. We're gon-na see Grand-ma and Grand-pa and my aunt and two cous-ins I don't like. I wish I was home, play-ing with my friends, go-ing swim-ming or rid-ing my bike. Yeah, I'm in the back seat, would-n't you know, my sis-ter's yell-ing in my ear, The ra-di-o's on, but it's Dad-dy's turn and he plays what I don't want to hear. We

words and music
© by Barry Louis Polisar

Everybody's screaming and poking at me; Timmy's got Tommy by the neck.
The dog is barking and he throws up too; Mom says we're gonna wreck.
My brother is yelling and pulling at me; He tries to climb over the seat.
My father swerves and slams on his brakes; I want something to eat.

chorus

Timmy and Tommy are rolling in the back; the dog jumps in Daddy's lap.
My mom is screaming (she's *really* mad), Dad's gonna have a heart attack.
My sister's crying, my Mom is yelling, my Daddy stops the car.
They say they'll make us get out and walk. Who do they think they are?

chorus

I Can't, I Can't

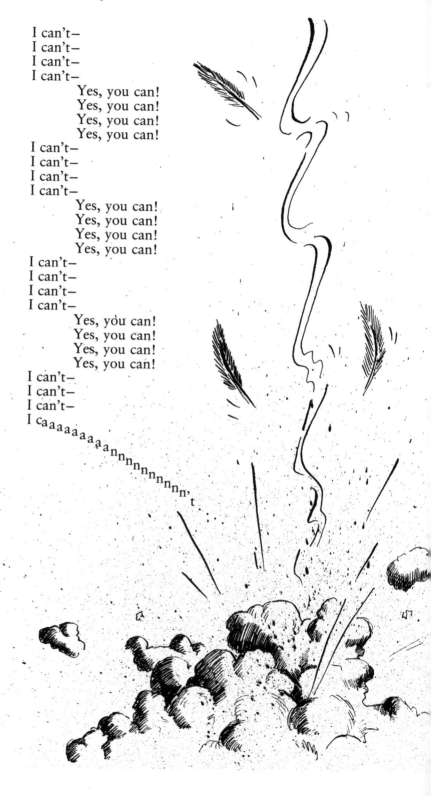

I can't–
I can't–
I can't–
I can't–
  Yes, you can!
  Yes, you can!
  Yes, you can!
  Yes, you can!
I can't–
I can't–
I can't–
I can't–
  Yes, you can!
  Yes, you can!
  Yes, you can!
  Yes, you can!
I can't–
I can't–
I can't–
I can't–
  Yes, you can!
  Yes, you can!
  Yes, you can!
  Yes, you can!
I can't–
I can't–
I can't–
I caaaaaaaaaannnnnnnnnnn't

I Wanna Be a Dog

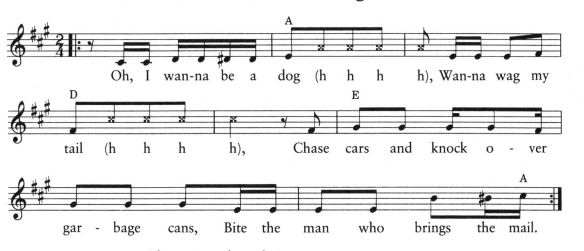

Oh, I wan-na be a dog (h h h h), Wan-na wag my
tail (h h h h), Chase cars and knock o - ver
gar - bage cans, Bite the man who brings the mail.

Oh, I wanna be a dog,
Wanna lie on the floor,
Chase squirels and cats, get fed, get fat,
Chew your shoe and bark at the door.

Oh, I wanna be a dog,
I wanna dig holes,
Flirt with French poodles and basset hounds
And pee on telephone poles.

Oh, I wanna be a dog,
Wanna drool on the ground
Scratch fleas and ticks and run after sticks,
I just wanna be a hound.

Oh, I wanna have dog breath
And wake the neighbors, too.
I'll like your hand, be the best friend to man,
Don't have nothing better to do.

Oh, I wanna be a dog,
I want my nose to be wet.
I've got a college degree but all I wanna be
Is somebody else's pet.

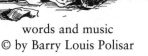

words and music
© by Barry Louis Polisar

I Don't Wanna Go to School

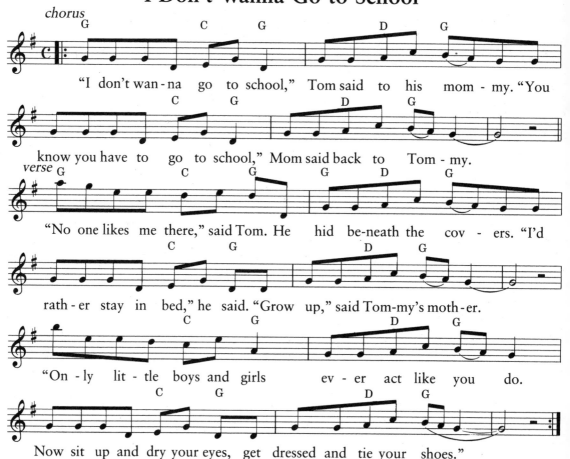

chorus

Tom ducked his head beneath the sheets
And kicked his feet about.
His mother heard him whimpering
And told him not to pout.

"I can't face another day,
The children are not nice."
She wiped his cheek and told him to
Follow her advice.

chorus

words and music
© by Barry Louis Polisar

"But people laugh at me at school,"
Tom told his mom again,
"The teachers will not talk to me,
I don't have any friends."

"Now Tom, get up," said Tommy's mom,
She hoped he was convincible.
"You've got to go to school," she said,
"Because you are the Principal."

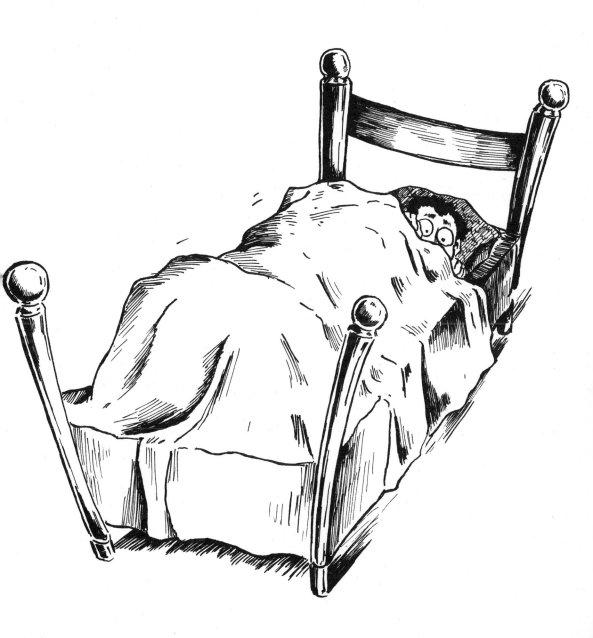

Underwear

Un - der - wear is ev - 'ry - where but most - ly un - der-neath,

Though, us - ual - ly you can't see what goes on be - neath

Rag - ged clothes or ev - 'ning gowns or the

fin - est three-piece suit. Un - der - wear is

ev - 'ry - where, there is no sub - sti - tute.

Ev - 'ry - one is e - qual when it

comes to un - der - wear, Be - cause be - neath your

un - der - wear it's just your - self that's there.

Ev - 'ry - one wears un - der - wear, or at least they

words and music
© by Barry Louis Polisar

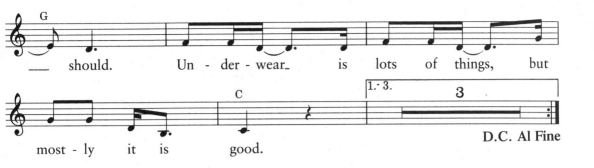

_ should. Un - der - wear_ is lots of things, but

most - ly it is good.

D.C. Al Fine

chorus

Some like the feel of cotton. I share this belief,
Likewise, I don't like boxer shorts, give me a pair of briefs.
Some don't like to talk about it—that's because they're shy,
People laugh at underwear, but I do not know why.

chorus

Now don't use bleach on underwear, that's what my mom will say,
'Cause bleach will eat the fabric and soon they'll wash away,
And underwear with lots of holes is a sorry sight,
Look around and try to see who's wearing theirs too tight!

chorus

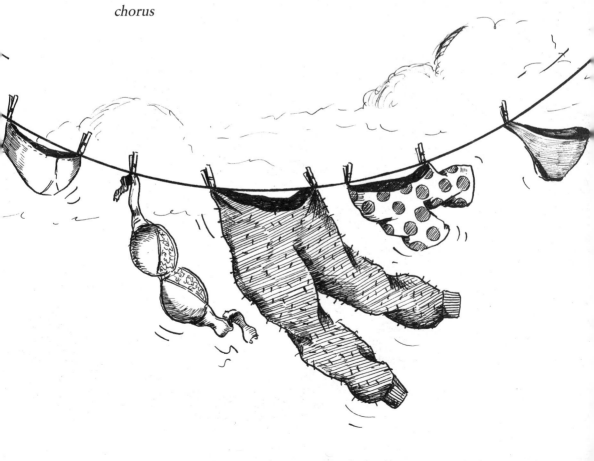

My Mother Ran Away Today

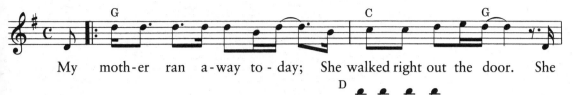

My moth-er ran a-way to-day; She walked right out the door. She

packed her tooth-brush and her pa-jam-as, said, "I can't take it no more." She

She said that she was tired,
She said she'd had her fill
Of cooking our meals, washing our clothes,
And cleaning all our spills.

She said she'd write us letters
With no return address,
She said that she'd come back someday,
But now she had to rest.

She took the plants, she took the cats,
Took our pictures from the wall,
And though it's only been two hours,
I wish that she would call.

I never thought I'd miss her,
Isn't that the way?
You never know how much Mom means to you,
Until she runs away.

words and music
© by Barry Louis Polisar

Thump, Thump, Thump

words and music
© by Barry Louis Polisar

Thump, thump, thump!

Then the lights went out.

Thump, thump, thump!   I be-gan to shout.   Thump, thump, thump!

It was getting close.
Thump, thump, thump!
I thought it was a ghost.
Thump, thump, thump!
I dove under the covers.
Thump, thump, thump!
I screamed for my mother.
Thump, thump, thump!
No one answered back.
Thump, thump, thump!
I was gonna be attacked.
Thump, thump, thump!
The door started creaking.
Thump, thump, thump!
Somebody was sneaking.
Thump, thump, thump!
I was screaming and a-hollerin'–
Thump, thump, thump!
And something was a-followin'–
Thump, thump, thump!
Me around the room.
Thump, thump, thump!
I hoped my parents came soon.
Thump, thump, thump!
I closed my eyes.
Thump, thump, thump!
I said, "I don't wanna die."
Thump, thump, thump!
What could it be
Thump, thump, thump!
Coming after me?
Thump, thump, thump!
I tried again to shout.
Thump, thump, thump!
I never found out!
Thump, thump, thump!

Nothing

"What did you do in school to-day?" "Noth-ing! Noth-ing!" Did
you say, "Noth-ing?" What did you say? "Noth-ing! Noth-ing!"
"Did-n't you work and study real hard?" "No, we sat out
in the yard." "Noth-ing?" "Noth-ing! Noth-ing!"

"What do you do when you don't go to school?"
"Nothing! Nothing!"
"But everybody's got something they do!"
"Nothing! Nothing!"
"Don't you have fun? Don't you ride your bikes?"
"We just sit around—there's nothing we like."
"Nothing?" "Nothing! Nothing!"

"What do you do when you see your friends?"
"Nothing! Nothing!"
"But you go to their houses again and again."
"Nothing! Nothing!"
"Don't you play games with other girls and boys?"
"We have no friends and we hate our toys."
"Nothing?" "Nothing! Nothing!"

"What did you do with yourself last summer?"
"Nothing! Nothing!"
"Every time you speak you sound dumber and dumber."
"Nothing! Nothing!"
"Didn't you swim and play on the swings?"
"Summer was a bummer and we didn't do a thing!"
"Nothing?" "Nothing! Nothing!"

"What will you do for the rest of your life?"
"Nothing! Nothing!"
"You've got to find something that you like!"
"Nothing! Nothing!"
"You can't sit around—it will drive you insane."
"You can if you don't have a brain"
"Nothing?" "Nothing! Nothing!"

words and music
© by Barry Louis Polisar

The Barry Louis Polisar Catalog

Current CDs:
Family Trip: Songs about Families
Old Dogs, New Tricks: Songs about Animals
Teacher's Favorites: Songs about School
Naughty Songs for Boys and Girls
Juggling Babies: Songs about Toddlers
Family Concert: A Concert Sampler
Barry Louis Polisar's A Little Different

Original Archival CD Recordings:
I Eat Kids and Other Songs for Rebellious Children (1975)
My Brother Thinks He's a Banana and Other Provocative Songs for Children (1977)
Captured Live and in the Act (1978)
Songs for Well Behaved Children (1979)
Stanley Stole My Shoelace and Rubbed It in His Armpit (1982)
Off-Color Songs for Kids (1983)

Books
Insect Soup: Bug Poems
Peculiar Zoo: Poems about Unusual Animals
The Trouble with Ben
The Snake Who Was Afraid of People
Snakes and the Boy Who Was Afraid of Them
The Haunted House Party
Dinosaurs I Have Known
Don't Do That: A Child's Guide to Bad Manners
A Little Less Noise

Noises From Under The Rug: The Barry Louis Polisar Songbook
© 1985 by Barry Louis Polisar
Revised Edition © 2005 by Barry Louis Polisar
All Songs © by Barry Louis Polisar 1975-1983
Published by Rainbow Morning Music
2121 Fairland Road, Silver Spring, Maryland 20904
www.barrylou.com
First Revised Edition
ISBN 0-938663-24-0